EMMANUEL JOSEPH

How To Excel As A Collage Fresher

Contents

1

Chapter 1: Welcome to College

Introduction: The Journey Begins

Starting college is an exciting and transformative experience. It's a time of new beginnings, opportunities, and challenges. In this chapter, we'll explore the transition from high school to college and how to set the right expectations and goals for your journey ahead.

The Transition

1.1 Saying Goodbye to High School: Leaving behind the familiar halls of high school can be both liberating and a bit overwhelming. You'll reflect on the memories you've created and the friends you're leaving behind. Embrace this transition as a natural part of growing up.

1.2 Expectations vs. Reality: College can be different from what you've seen in movies or heard from older siblings. It's important to manage your expectations and understand that it's okay not to have everything figured out from day one. This chapter will help you adjust to the realities of college life.

Setting Goals and Intentions

1.3 Defining Your Goals: College is a time to explore your passions and shape your future. We'll discuss how to set both short-term and long-term goals, whether they're academic, personal, or career-oriented. Goal setting provides a roadmap for your college journey.

1.4 Academic and Personal Growth: College isn't just about gaining academic knowledge; it's about personal growth too. We'll explore the skills and qualities that you can develop during your time in college and how they can contribute to your success.

Building Resilience and Adaptability

1.5 Embracing Change: College is a dynamic environment where change is constant. Learn to adapt to different circumstances, whether it's adapting to a new city, making new friends, or dealing with challenging courses.

1.6 Building Resilience: Resilience is your ability to bounce back from setbacks. We'll provide strategies to cope with academic and personal challenges, helping you build a strong foundation for success.

Setting a Positive Mindset

1.7 The Power of a Positive Mindset: Your mindset plays a significant role in your college experience. We'll discuss the benefits of maintaining a positive attitude, embracing a growth mindset, and staying motivated throughout your journey.

Conclusion: A Fresh Start

As you embark on this new chapter of your life, remember that college is an incredible opportunity for personal and academic growth. Embrace the changes, set meaningful goals, and maintain a positive mindset. In the chapters to come, we'll delve deeper into the essential skills and strategies to excel as a college freshman. Your journey is just beginning, and the possibilities are endless.

2

Chapter 2: Time Management

Mastering the Art of Time Management

College life can be a whirlwind of classes, assignments, social activities, and more. To excel as a college freshman, you need to become a master of time management. In this chapter, we'll explore the crucial skills and techniques to help you make the most of your time.

The Importance of Time Management

2.1 Why Time Management Matters: Understand the significance of effective time management in college. It can reduce stress, improve your academic performance, and provide you with valuable free time.

2.2 Identifying Time Wasters: Recognize common time-wasting habits and learn how to overcome them. Identify distractions and create strategies to eliminate them.

Creating a College Schedule

2.3 Creating a Weekly Schedule: Learn how to build a flexible weekly schedule that includes your classes, study time, extracurricular activities, and personal commitments. We'll provide templates and tips for crafting a well-balanced calendar.

2.4 Setting Priorities: Prioritize your tasks and responsibilities. Understand the difference between urgent and important activities, and focus on what truly matters.

Balancing Academics and Social Life

2.5 The Art of Balance: Achieving a balance between your academic and social life is essential. We'll guide you in finding equilibrium, ensuring you don't miss out on social experiences while excelling academically.

2.6 Effective Goal Setting: Use your time management skills to set academic and personal goals. We'll explore SMART goals (Specific, Measurable, Achievable, Relevant, Time-bound) and how to apply them to your college life.

Tools and Techniques

2.7 Time Management Tools: Discover various tools and technologies that can aid in time management, including apps, planners, and digital calendars. Find the tools that work best for your needs.

2.8 Time Management Techniques: Dive into proven techniques such as the Pomodoro Technique, time blocking, and the Eisenhower Matrix. We'll help you choose the methods that suit your personal style.

Avoiding Burnout

2.9 Recognizing Burnout Signs: Understand the signs of burnout and how to prevent it. Learn the importance of self-care and how to maintain a healthy work-life balance.

Conclusion: Your Time, Your Success

Effective time management is a key to success in college. With the skills and strategies covered in this chapter, you'll be better equipped to handle your responsibilities, make the most of your time, and enjoy a well-rounded college experience. In the upcoming chapters, we'll explore study techniques and academic success strategies to complement your time management skills. Remember, your time is a valuable resource—use it wisely.

3

Chapter 3: Study Skills

The Foundation of Academic Success

As a college freshman, your academic performance is crucial. To excel in your studies, you need effective study skills. In this chapter, we'll explore various techniques and strategies to help you become a more efficient and successful student.

Effective Study Techniques

3.1 Active Learning: Understand the power of active learning. We'll cover techniques such as summarization, self-testing, and concept mapping, which engage your brain and improve retention.

3.2 Effective Note-Taking: Learn the art of note-taking. Discover different methods, including the Cornell method, the outline method, and digital note-taking. We'll also discuss how to take notes during lectures and while reading textbooks.

Organization and Time Management for Studying

3.3 Study Environment: Create a productive study environment that minimizes distractions and maximizes focus. We'll offer tips on setting up a study space that works for you.

3.4 Time Management for Study: We'll expand on the time management skills discussed in Chapter 2, focusing on how to allocate your study time effectively and avoid procrastination.

Improving Memory and Retention

3.5 Memory Techniques: Explore memory-enhancing techniques such as mnemonic devices, spaced repetition, and visualization. These methods can help you remember information more effectively.

Research and Information Gathering

3.6 Library and Online Research: Navigate the college library and online databases for research projects. We'll guide you through finding credible sources and evaluating information for academic assignments.

Test Preparation and Exam Strategies

3.7 Test-Taking Strategies: Get ready for exams with effective test preparation techniques, including practice tests, time management during exams, and strategies for multiple-choice and essay questions.

3.8 Managing Test Anxiety: Learn to manage test anxiety and stress. We'll provide relaxation techniques and mindfulness exercises to help you stay calm during exams.

Group Study and Collaboration

3.9 Collaborative Learning: Discover the benefits of group study and effective ways to collaborate with your peers for a deeper understanding of your coursework.

Conclusion: Mastery of Learning

Your study skills are the foundation of your academic success in college. By implementing the techniques and strategies discussed in this chapter, you can become a more efficient and effective learner. In the upcoming chapters, we'll continue to explore strategies for excelling academically, from acing exams to writing papers and managing your academic workload. Remember, learning is a lifelong skill, and it's never too early to refine your approach.

4

Chapter 4: Building Relationships

Connecting in College

College is not just about academics; it's also an opportunity to build lasting relationships and connections. In this chapter, we'll explore how to make friends, navigate roommate relationships, and become an active member of your college community.

Making Friends and Connections

4.1 The Importance of Social Connections: Understand the significance of building a support network in college. We'll discuss the benefits of friendships, both academically and personally.

4.2 Initiating Conversations: Learn effective strategies for starting conversations and making new friends. We'll provide tips for approaching people, joining social events, and participating in campus activities.

Navigating Roommates and Dorm Life

4.3 Living with Roommates: For many college freshmen, living with a roommate is a new experience. We'll offer guidance on effective communication, setting boundaries, and resolving conflicts with roommates.

4.4 Dorm Life and Community: Make the most of your dormitory experience. We'll explore ways to engage with your dorm community, participate in residence hall activities, and create a comfortable living space.

Joining Clubs and Organizations

4.5 Extracurricular Involvement: Discover the wide range of clubs, organizations, and extracurricular activities available on campus. Learn how to find the right ones for you and make the most of your involvement.

4.6 Leadership Opportunities: Explore how to take on leadership roles within clubs and organizations. Leadership experience can enhance your college experience and future career prospects.

Building Inclusive Relationships

4.7 Embracing Diversity: College campuses are often diverse and inclusive environments. We'll discuss the importance of respecting and embracing diversity and provide tips on building relationships across cultures.

4.8 Conflict Resolution: Learn effective conflict resolution strategies for maintaining healthy relationships with peers. We'll cover communication techniques and approaches to handle disagreements.

Professional Relationships

4.9 Faculty and Advisor Relationships: Build positive relationships with professors and academic advisors. These connections can provide academic support, guidance, and opportunities for research or internships.

Conclusion: A Rich Social Tapestry

College is not just about education but also about forming meaningful relationships. By following the advice and strategies in this chapter, you'll be better equipped to make friends, navigate living arrangements, and build inclusive and professional relationships. These connections will enrich your college experience and support your personal and academic growth. In the chapters to come, we'll delve into maintaining wellness and self-care, ensuring that you have a strong foundation for success both academically and personally.

5

Chapter 5: Wellness and Self-Care

Prioritizing Your Well-Being

As you embark on your college journey, it's essential to prioritize your physical and mental well-being. In this chapter, we'll explore strategies for managing stress, maintaining your mental health, and taking care of your overall wellness.

Managing Stress and Mental Health

5.1 Understanding Stress: Recognize the signs of stress and the impact it can have on your academic and personal life. We'll discuss the sources of stress in college and how to manage them effectively.

5.2 Stress Management Techniques: Learn various stress-reduction techniques, including mindfulness, meditation, and physical activity. Discover how to create a personalized stress management plan.

Maintaining Physical Health

5.3 Physical Wellness: Explore the importance of regular exercise, nutrition, and sleep in maintaining physical health. We'll provide tips for fitting physical wellness into your busy college schedule.

5.4 Nutrition and Eating Habits: Make informed choices about your diet. Understand the importance of balanced nutrition and how it can impact your energy and cognitive function.

Sleep and Time Management for Wellness

5.5 The Value of Sleep: Learn about the significance of quality sleep for your well-being and academic performance. We'll discuss sleep hygiene and how to establish a sleep routine.

5.6 Balancing Sleep and Study: Balance your academic responsibilities with adequate sleep. Discover effective time management techniques to ensure you get enough rest while excelling in your studies.

Seeking Support and Counseling

5.7 Counseling Services: Understand the counseling and mental health services available on campus. Learn how to access these resources and the importance of seeking help when needed.

5.8 Support Systems: Cultivate a support system of friends, family, and mentors. We'll discuss the value of open communication and seeking support when facing challenges.

Personal Wellness Practices

5.9 Self-Care Routine: Develop a personalized self-care routine that aligns with your interests and needs. This can include hobbies, relaxation activities, and spending time with loved ones.

Conclusion: Your Well-Being Matters

Your well-being is the foundation of your success in college. By focusing on stress management, physical health, and self-care, you'll be better prepared to handle the demands of college life while maintaining a balanced and healthy lifestyle. In the upcoming chapters, we'll continue to explore academic success strategies and financial responsibility, ensuring that you have a well-rounded foundation for excelling as a college freshman. Remember, taking care of yourself is an essential part of your college journey.

6

Chapter 6: Academic Success

Achieving Excellence in Your Studies

As a college freshman, your primary focus is on academics. This chapter will delve into strategies to excel academically, including choosing the right classes and major, utilizing campus resources, and achieving success in exams and assignments.

Choosing the Right Classes and Major

6.1 Academic Advising: Learn how to work with academic advisors to choose the right classes and create a balanced course schedule.

6.2 Exploring Majors: Understand the process of choosing a major. We'll discuss the importance of exploring your interests and long-term career goals.

Utilizing Campus Resources

6.3 Library and Research Resources: Explore the wealth of research resources available on campus, including libraries, databases, and academic journals.

6.4 Academic Support Services: Discover the various academic support services offered, such as tutoring, writing centers, and study groups. These resources can enhance your understanding of coursework.

Effective Study Techniques

6.5 Exam Preparation: Learn how to prepare for exams effectively. We'll cover techniques for creating study guides, using flashcards, and staying organized.

6.6 Acing Assignments: Excel in written assignments by mastering the writing process. We'll provide tips for research, outlining, and editing essays and papers.

Time Management for Academic Success

6.7 Academic Time Management: Apply advanced time management skills specifically tailored to your academic workload. We'll discuss creating an academic calendar and staying on top of assignments and deadlines.

6.8 Balancing Coursework: Understand how to balance the demands of multiple courses by prioritizing tasks and using study schedules.

Evaluating Your Progress

6.9 Self-Assessment: Continuously assess your academic progress. Understand how to gauge your understanding of the material and identify areas where you need to improve.

Conclusion: A Foundation for Excellence

This chapter has equipped you with the tools and strategies needed for academic success in college. By selecting the right courses, utilizing campus resources, and mastering study techniques, you'll be on the path to achieving excellence in your studies. In the upcoming chapters, we'll explore financial responsibility, effective communication skills, and setting career goals. Academic success is an essential part of your college journey, and with the right strategies, you can excel in your coursework and set the stage for a successful future.

7

Chapter 7: Financial Responsibility

Navigating Financial Independence

As a college freshman, you may be experiencing greater financial independence. This chapter will guide you in understanding financial responsibility, budgeting for college life, managing student loans, and exploring part-time jobs and internships.

Budgeting for College Life

7.1 Financial Planning: Understand the importance of financial planning in college. We'll guide you in setting up a budget to manage your expenses, including tuition, housing, textbooks, and daily living costs.

7.2 Creating a Budget: Learn how to create a realistic and effective budget that considers income, expenses, and savings goals. We'll discuss budgeting apps and tools that can help you stay on track.

Understanding Student Loans and Debt

7.3 Student Loans 101: Gain a comprehensive understanding of student loans, including federal and private loans. We'll explore the FAFSA application process and explain the terms and conditions of student loans.

7.4 Debt Management: Discover strategies for managing student loan debt effectively, including options for repayment plans and loan forgiveness programs.

Part-Time Jobs and Internships

7.5 Part-Time Employment: Explore the benefits of part-time jobs in college, including gaining work experience, building your resume, and contributing to your finances.

7.6 Internship Opportunities: Understand the significance of internships in building a strong career foundation. We'll discuss how to search for internships and make the most of these opportunities.

Financial Literacy and Savings

7.7 Financial Literacy: Improve your financial literacy by understanding concepts such as credit, investments, and taxes. We'll provide resources to help you become a financially informed student.

7.8 Savings Strategies: Learn how to develop a savings plan for both short-term and long-term goals. We'll explore the power of compounding interest and smart savings practices.

Conclusion: Financial Freedom and Responsibility

Financial responsibility is a crucial aspect of your college experience. This chapter has equipped you with the knowledge and tools to manage your finances effectively, from creating a budget to understanding student loans and exploring job opportunities. In the upcoming chapters, we'll delve into effective communication skills, setting career goals, and embracing diversity and inclusivity on campus. Financial stability is an essential component of your college journey, and with the right strategies, you can achieve your academic and financial goals.

8

Chapter 8: Communication Skills

The Art of Effective Communication

Communication is a cornerstone of success, both in college and beyond. In this chapter, we'll explore strategies for communicating effectively with professors, networking, and building positive relationships.

Effective Communication with Professors

8.1 Building Rapport: Understand the importance of establishing a positive relationship with your professors. Learn how to introduce yourself, ask questions, and seek academic guidance.

8.2 Office Hours: Explore the benefits of attending professors' office hours. We'll provide tips on how to make the most of these opportunities for one-on-one interaction.

Networking and Building Professional Relationships

8.3 Networking Skills: Develop networking skills that will serve you well in college and future career endeavors. We'll discuss the art of networking, both on and off campus.

8.4 LinkedIn and Online Presence: Learn how to create a professional online presence through platforms like LinkedIn. Discover the value of online networking and personal branding.

Conflict Resolution and Effective Feedback

8.5 Conflict Resolution: Gain insights into conflict resolution techniques. We'll cover how to address disagreements and misunderstandings professionally.

8.6 Receiving and Giving Feedback: Master the art of giving and receiving constructive feedback. Understand how feedback can lead to personal and academic growth.

Written and Oral Communication Skills

8.7 Written Communication: Explore strategies for improving your written communication skills, whether through emails, essays, or reports. Learn how to convey your ideas effectively.

8.8 Oral Communication: Enhance your oral communication skills, including public speaking and presentation techniques. We'll provide tips for overcoming stage fright and delivering impactful speeches.

Conclusion: Building Bridges with Effective Communication

Effective communication is a vital skill that will serve you well throughout your college journey and beyond. By mastering the strategies discussed in this chapter, you'll be better equipped to connect with professors, build professional relationships, and navigate communication challenges. In the upcoming chapters, we'll explore setting career goals, embracing diversity and inclusivity, and making the most of your college life. Remember, strong communication skills are a valuable asset that can open doors to opportunities in both your personal and professional life.

9

Chapter 9: Setting Career Goals

Navigating Your Future

College is a time to explore your interests, gain skills, and set the stage for your future career. In this chapter, we'll explore the process of setting and achieving your career goals, including exploring different career options and securing internships.

Exploring Career Options

9.1 Self-Exploration: Understand your interests, strengths, and values. We'll discuss self-assessment tools and how they can guide your career exploration.

9.2 Career Counseling: Learn how to work with career counselors and utilize on-campus resources to help you explore potential career paths.

Securing Internships and Co-op Programs

9.3 Internship Search: Discover strategies for finding internships and co-op programs that align with your career goals. We'll discuss how to search for opportunities, craft a strong resume, and prepare for interviews.

9.4 Maximizing Internships: Once you secure an internship, learn how to make the most of the experience. We'll discuss the importance of networking, setting goals, and gaining valuable skills during your internship.

Professional Development

9.5 Professional Development Workshops: Take advantage of professional development workshops and events on campus. We'll discuss the value of attending workshops, seminars, and career fairs.

9.6 Resume Building: Craft a powerful resume that showcases your skills, experiences, and accomplishments. We'll provide tips for tailoring your resume to specific career goals.

Setting Long-Term Career Goals

9.7 Setting SMART Career Goals: Develop clear, specific, and achievable long-term career goals. We'll explore how SMART (Specific, Measurable, Achievable, Relevant, Time-bound) goals can guide your professional journey.

9.8 Career Planning: Create a career plan that outlines the steps required to reach your long-term goals. We'll discuss the importance of adaptability in your career path.

Conclusion: A Path to Success

Your college journey is a significant step toward your future career. By following the advice and strategies in this chapter, you'll be better equipped to explore your career options, secure internships, and set meaningful long-term goals. In the upcoming chapters, we'll explore making the most of your college life, embracing diversity and inclusivity, and preparing for life after college. Remember, your time in college is an opportunity to shape your future, and with the right strategies, you can build a strong foundation for success.

10

Chapter 10: Diversity and Inclusivity

Embracing Diversity and Inclusivity

College campuses are often vibrant and diverse communities, and embracing this diversity is crucial for personal growth and a positive college experience. In this chapter, we'll explore the importance of diversity, inclusivity, and cultural sensitivity in college life.

Understanding Diversity

10.1 Diversity in College: Understand the various forms of diversity you may encounter on campus, including cultural, racial, religious, and socioeconomic diversity.

10.2 The Benefits of Diversity: Explore the advantages of diverse perspectives and backgrounds in education and personal growth.

Promoting Inclusivity

10.3 Inclusivity on Campus: Discover the initiatives and organizations that promote inclusivity and equal opportunities on campus.

10.4 Your Role in Inclusivity: Learn how you can contribute to creating an inclusive campus environment. We'll discuss being an ally and taking part in inclusivity efforts.

Cultural Sensitivity

10.5 Cultural Competence: Develop cultural competence by gaining knowledge of different cultures, traditions, and perspectives.

10.6 Avoiding Stereotypes and Prejudice: Understand the importance of avoiding stereotypes and prejudice. We'll discuss how to challenge and address biases.

Respectful Communication and Engagement

10.7 Respectful Communication: Learn the art of respectful communication with individuals from diverse backgrounds. We'll provide tips for engaging in conversations that foster understanding and respect.

10.8 Participation in Cultural Activities: Engage in cultural events, activities, and organizations on campus. These experiences can broaden your understanding and appreciation of different cultures.

Conclusion: Embracing a Diverse World

College is an opportunity to interact with people from diverse backgrounds and develop a greater understanding of the world. By embracing diversity, promoting inclusivity, and practicing cultural sensitivity, you'll be better prepared to navigate a globalized society and make meaningful connections during your college journey. In the upcoming chapters, we'll explore making the most of your college life, preparing for graduation, and post-college options. Remember, the lessons you learn about diversity and inclusivity are valuable and will serve you well in your future personal and professional interactions.

11

Chapter 11: Making the Most of College Life

A Well-Rounded College Experience

College isn't just about classes and studying; it's a time to explore your interests, engage with your community, and create lifelong memories. In this chapter, we'll explore how to make the most of your college life through extracurricular activities, study abroad programs, and personal growth opportunities.

Getting Involved in Extracurricular Activities

11.1 Exploring Interests: Discover clubs, organizations, and extracurricular activities that align with your passions and interests. We'll discuss the benefits of getting involved.

11.2 Time Management for Extracurriculars: Learn how to balance your academic commitments with extracurricular involvement. Effective time management is crucial to thriving in both areas.

Exploring Your Interests

11.3 Exploring Hobbies and Interests: Beyond structured clubs, take time to explore your personal interests and hobbies. These activities can provide balance and relaxation.

11.4 Staying Active: Understand the importance of physical activity and how to incorporate it into your daily life. We'll discuss campus fitness facilities, sports, and outdoor activities.

Studying Abroad and Travel Opportunities

11.5 Studying Abroad Programs: Explore the benefits of studying abroad, including personal growth, cultural exposure, and academic enrichment.

11.6 Travel Experiences: Consider travel opportunities, whether through study programs or independent exploration. We'll discuss the value of experiencing different cultures and perspectives.

Leadership and Personal Growth

11.7 Leadership Roles: Discover the personal growth opportunities that leadership roles within clubs and organizations can offer. We'll discuss how leadership skills can enhance your college experience.

11.8 Mentorship and Networking: Build meaningful connections with mentors, peers, and alumni. Networking is a valuable aspect of personal and professional growth.

Conclusion: A Fulfilling College Experience

Your college journey is a unique and transformative time in your life. By making the most of your college life through extracurricular activities, exploring your interests, and seeking personal growth opportunities, you'll create lasting memories and develop a well-rounded foundation for your future. In the upcoming chapters, we'll explore preparing for your senior year, graduation, and life after college. Remember, college is not just about academics; it's also about personal and social growth. Enjoy every moment of this special time in your life.

12

Chapter 12: Preparing for the Future

The Next Chapter Begins

As your college journey comes to an end, it's time to focus on preparing for the future. This chapter will guide you through senior year and graduation planning, post-graduation options, and life after college.

Senior Year and Graduation Planning

12.1 Academic Checkup: Review your academic progress and ensure you're on track to meet graduation requirements. We'll discuss the importance of meeting with academic advisors.

12.2 Capstone Projects: If required by your program, explore capstone projects, senior theses, or final presentations. We'll provide tips for managing these comprehensive projects.

Post-Graduation Options

12.3 Job Search: Learn effective strategies for job searching, including crafting resumes, writing cover letters, and preparing for interviews.

12.4 Graduate School Planning: If you're considering graduate school, we'll explore the application process, including preparing for standardized tests and securing letters of recommendation.

Life After College

12.5 Financial Planning: Understand how to manage your finances after college. We'll discuss budgeting, student loan repayment, and building an emergency fund.

12.6 Life Transitions: Prepare for life transitions, including moving, finding housing, and adjusting to a new routine.

Embracing Your Future

12.7 Setting Career Goals: Continue setting and revising your long-term career goals as you transition into the workforce or graduate school.

12.8 Networking Post-Graduation: Understand the importance of networking even after college. We'll discuss how to maintain connections and build a strong professional network.

Conclusion: A Bright Future Awaits

College has been a transformative journey, and it's now time to embark on the next chapter of your life. By preparing for senior year, exploring post-graduation options, and planning for life after college, you'll be well-equipped for the future. Remember, your college experience has equipped you with valuable skills and knowledge, and the opportunities ahead are endless. Enjoy the excitement and possibilities that await you in your post-college journey.